YOUR LEGAL RIGHTS IN SCHOOL

REBECCA KLEIN

ROSEN
PUBLISHING

New York

Published in 2015 by The Rosen Publishing Group, Inc.
29 East 21st Street, New York, NY 10010

Expert Reviewer: Lindsay A. Lewis, Esq.

Library of Congress Cataloging-in-Publication Data

Klein, Rebecca T., author.
Your legal rights in school/Rebecca T. Klein.–First edition
    pages cm.—(Know your rights)
Includes bibliographical references and index.
ISBN 978-1-4777-8048-0 (library bound)—ISBN 978-1-4777-8049-7 (pbk.)—ISBN 978-1-4777-8050-3 (6-pack)
1. Civil rights—United States—Juvenile literature. 2. Discrimination in education—Law and legislation—United States—Juvenile literature. 3. Segregation in education—Law and legislation—United States—Juvenile literature. 4. Educational equalization—United States—Juvenile literature. I. Title.
KF4749.K54 2015
342.7308'5083—dc 3
                                                    2014021407

Manufactured in the United States of America

CONTENTS

INTRODUCTION

As a student, no matter how limited or extensive your experience with school rules and discipline, you probably wonder from time to time about your legal rights. It can be difficult to distinguish between the law and the rules implemented by your particular school. Sometimes, situations arise in which you feel that the rules, or at least the ways in which the rules are being enforced, are unfair. When this happens, you might feel as though you have no recourse and no power to change the situation. That simply isn't true. If a school rule or a disciplinary action truly violates your rights, you can do something about it. The key is to know your rights in relation to the issue at hand, or at least know how and where to find information about those rights.

The bad news is that there is no simple and comprehensive bill of rights for students—yet. However, that does not mean that there is no legal protection for students. Thanks to the Supreme Court's ruling in a case called *Tinker v. Des Moines*, the law supports the upholding of students' constitutional rights within the school system.

In 1965, three students in the Des Moines school system, John F. Tinker (fifteen), Mary Beth Tinker (thirteen), and Christopher Eckhardt (sixteen), developed a plan to wear armbands to school in protest of the Vietnam War. The school district learned of their plan and, in response, issued a policy stating that students could not wear armbands and could be suspended for refusing to remove them. The three students wore armbands anyway, and they were suspended. They petitioned the district court, which ruled that the school's policy was legal because

At age sixty-one, Mary Beth Tinker displays a photo of herself and her brother John with the now-famous armbands they fought for the right to wear in Tinker v. Des Moines, *a landmark case in students' rights.*

the wearing of armbands could potentially cause a disturbance.

Afterward, however, the Supreme Court overturned that decision, stating that the students' right to wear armbands was protected under the First Amendment, which guarantees free speech. "It can hardly be argued," reads the Court's decision, "that either students or teachers shed their constitutional rights at the schoolhouse gate." The decision goes on to discuss how important it is for citizens,

The Supreme Court ruled in Tinker v. Des Moines *that students and teachers do not "shed their constitutional rights at the schoolhouse gate" but retain those rights while in school.*

including students, to be able to express and discuss dissenting opinions. Free speech is only one of the rights protected under the Constitution. It also protects the rights of citizens, including students, to live lives free from discrimination and to receive due process regarding legal matters.

If a school policy or the actions of someone in authority violates those rights, it is usually up to the student to speak up and challenge that policy or action on legal grounds. The specific applications of the laws can also differ from state to state. This book will help to inform you of your rights as a student in many situations that you might encounter at school and give you an idea of some of the variations in the laws of different states. It will share stories of students who have been affected by and challenged questionable policies. It will help you to learn how to protect yourself from legal trouble, and it will also help to empower you if you find your own rights being violated.

CHAPTER 1

EXPRESS YOURSELF! THE RIGHT TO FREE SPEECH AND PEACEABLE ASSEMBLY

As the Supreme Court's decision in *Tinker v. Des Moines* determined, students have the right to free speech when they are at school. However, the decision also states that this right is guaranteed only if the expression of speech does not create a significant disruption to the school's functioning and to the learning of others. The students who wore armbands to school in Des Moines in 1965 did not intend to create a disturbance. They were simply expressing their views. The district court decided that because those views were outside of the mainstream, they had the potential to cause a disruption. The Supreme Court, however, ruled that this perceived potential was not reason enough to ban the armbands or to punish the students for wearing them.

What does this mean for you as a student when you want to exercise your right to free speech? It means that although that right is guaranteed, you have to be wise and strategic in the ways you choose to exercise it. For instance, if an instructor is teaching something with which you disagree or advocating a view that is different from your own, you absolutely have the right to speak up and express your opinion. However, you do not have the right to create a huge scene, yell or swear at the teacher, or try to rile up the rest of the class. You want to be sure that you speak up in such a way that you protect yourself from disciplinary action. If you conduct yourself peacefully and within legal boundaries, and someone tries to silence you, you have legal grounds to challenge that person. If you disrupt class, however, you are giving up your rights by giving the teacher fair reason to take disciplinary action.

Another important issue to address when discussing free speech is the content of that speech itself. In addition to not having the right to disrupt class or harass the teacher, you also do not have the right to harass your fellow students through written or verbal means. Although the law is somewhat murky regarding the definition of "hate speech," and although words that do not actively seek to incite violence cannot be deemed illegal, there are many ways in which hate speech could lead to legal or disciplinary consequences. Generally, speech that persecutes your fellow students could be considered verbal bullying. If that persecution is based on race, religion, or any other category protected by law, it qualifies as harassment and is illegal. A later section of this material will deal more extensively with bullying and harassment and the possible legal consequences of these actions.

PEACEABLE ASSEMBLY

In addition to free speech, the First Amendment also guarantees citizens the right to "peaceably assemble." This means exactly what it sounds like—people have the right to gather together in groups as long as they do so peacefully.

SEE YOU AT THE POLE AND PRAYER IN SCHOOLS

In recent history, there has been much debate about prayer in schools. This debate stems from interpretations of two clauses in the First Amendment. The first is the Establishment clause, which says that the state (which covers government institutions including public schools) may not declare a national religion, nor may it show preference for one religion over another. The second is the Free Exercise clause, which says that the government cannot prohibit the practice of any religion. Both sides of the debate have used varying interpretations of these clauses to argue that prayer in schools should either be banned or allowed.

See You at the Pole is a Christian movement that organizes students to gather at school flagpoles and pray on the fourth Wednesday in September. These gatherings usually take place before school and always take place outside of the times when students are required to be in class. They are organized by students themselves, and they are not endorsed or sponsored by the schools. The organization's website references guidelines established by President Bill Clinton in 1990, which read: "Students may also participate in before or after school events with religious content, such as 'see you at the flagpole' gatherings, on the same terms as they may participate in other non-curriculum activities on school premises. School officials may neither discourage nor encourage participation in such an event."

See You at the Pole gatherings are legal under the First Amendment precisely because the schools neither endorse nor prohibit them. These students are guaranteed the right to exercise their religion, which includes praying. However, schools are absolutely not allowed to require prayer or to endorse any particular religion over another. This means, for instance, that Muslim students who wish to pray throughout

A group of students gathers for See You at the Pole, a religious assembly that is constitutionally protected because it takes place before school hours and is not endorsed by schools.

the day must be allowed to do so. In their role as extensions of the government, public schools must follow the same rules set up in the Establishment clause and the Free Exercise clause. They must allow all students the freedom to practice their religions, and they may not show preference for any one religion.

This right has been integral to many political movements in the United States, including the abolitionist movement, which sought to make slavery illegal, the civil rights movement, which fought against segregation, and the women's suffrage movement, which sought the right to vote for women. Each of these movements relied heavily on the people's right to gather for parades, marches, and rallies, as have many large and small movements in recent times.

As a student, you have the right to gather together with your fellow students to express your support for something or your dissent against it. However, just as you have to be wise when exercising your right to free speech, you also have to be wise when organizing any kind of assembly. The group that gathers must remain peaceful and may not engage in any violence or destruction of property.

There are many different reasons why students might want to peacefully assemble. Perhaps you want to show support for a cause in the news, such as marriage equality or affordable health care. Perhaps you want to protest a political action, like the

The women's suffrage movement relied heavily on the right to peaceably assemble for its marches and gatherings, which eventually won American women the right to vote in 1920.

students involved in *Tinker v. Des Moines* protested the war in Vietnam. Perhaps you want to protest a school policy that you feel is unfair or show support for a fellow student you feel is being treated unjustly. Each of these circumstances provides possible reasons for assembling a peaceful group of students who share the same sentiment.

If you wish to gather a group of students for a peaceable assembly, you should take some precautions to make sure that you are operating within your rights as a student. First of all, you should make sure that the location and time you have chosen for the assembly does not disrupt the school's functioning or your fellow classmates' learning. This can be frustrating because you might feel that disrupting the day-to-day procedures is the only way to draw attention to your cause. However, you should weigh the possible consequences against the effects that your protest might have. Is it really worthwhile to put yourself at the risk of legal or disciplinary action? If you decide that it is, you should prepare yourself for everything that might happen as a result of your decision.

You should also consider finding a way to express your views without putting yourself at risk. For instance, organize a gathering during lunch or before or after school hours that takes place on school grounds but does not affect the school's day-to-day operations or other students' learning. You should also be very careful to make it clear to all students who choose to participate that they may not engage in any sort of violence or destruction of property. This way, if school personnel try to accuse you of a violation, you can argue that your actions were within your constitutional rights.

It is important to keep in mind that you cannot control the actions of other students who choose to participate in an event that you have organized. As the organizer of an event, you may be held responsible for those actions.

Therefore, before making plans for a protest or a gathering, you should carefully evaluate the situation and seek out protections against unforeseen circumstances and potential consequences, and try to protect yourself against these risks in advance.

It is important to be aware that each school district and/or individual school may have its own rules and policies regarding speech and assembly. If you do something that is in violation of the school's code of conduct, especially if you or your parent has signed that code of conduct, you will probably be subject to disciplinary action, even if you were acting within your constitutional rights. However, knowing your rights can be helpful in challenging that disciplinary action. You can make it clear that you were careful to operate within legal guidelines, which might help to persuade school officials to be more lenient.

If you truly feel that a school policy has violated your rights, you can seek the assistance of an organization that provides legal assistance regarding civil-rights issues, such as the American Civil Liberties Union (ACLU). However, it is important to be aware that these organizations receive many similar requests every year, so there is no guarantee that they can take on your case. It is certainly worthwhile to try, but you should also be prepared to hire a lawyer.

It is not simple or easy to challenge school policies, but it definitely has been done successfully in many cases. If you are careful to research your rights, and to operate within those rights in the first place, you will have solid legal grounds on which to stand when challenging rules that violate those rights.

CHAPTER 2

LIBERTY AND JUSTICE FOR ALL: FREEDOM FROM DISCRIMINATION

When the Constitution was originally drafted in 1787, the rights it guaranteed were afforded only to certain people. In general, those people were white men. Over time, as the nation changed, the Constitution was amended to extend these rights to other groups, including African Americans and women. The Fourteenth Amendment was the first legislation that prohibited discrimination. Although it does not explicitly mention race, it reads: "All persons born or naturalized in the United States, and subject to the jurisdiction thereof, are citizens of the United States and of the state in which they reside. No state shall make or enforce any law which shall abridge the privileges or immunities of citizens of the United States; nor shall any state deprive any person of life, liberty, or property without due process of law; nor deny to any person within its jurisdiction the equal protection of the laws."

This amendment was added after the Civil War and guaranteed constitutional rights and citizenship to the newly freed African-American population. However, the

The Constitution was drafted and signed in 1787, but it established rights for only certain people. Its original text has been amended several times to extend and improve upon the rights it guarantees.

next hundred years proved that the Fourteenth Amendment was not enough to prevent discrimination. In the South, reactionary state governments passed Jim Crow laws that mandated separate facilities for black citizens in almost every facet of life. Although the North did not have explicit laws encouraging discrimination, there was certainly bias in everything from hiring practices to law enforcement. Throughout the late 1950s and early 1960s, African Americans and their allies began to fight for an end to discriminatory policies and for additional legislation to prevent them. This fight gave rise to the Civil Rights Act of 1964, a law that explicitly prohibits employers from discrimination on the basis of race or gender in relation to hiring, firing, and compensating employees. Subsequently, other categories have been added to those protected under the Civil Rights

Act, including creed (religion), color (which is sometimes perceived differently from race), and national origin.

DRESS CODE, SPORTS, AND DISCRIMINATION

Any time your constitutional rights, such as freedom of speech and freedom of expression, are violated, you have a right to challenge that violation. However, if rules and policies that violate those rights are applied disproportionately based upon your race, religion, nationality, or gender, then you have even more specific grounds on which to protest.

For instance, if a dress code policy prevents you from wearing clothing that is part of your religion, you can argue that this policy is discriminatory. All students have the right to wear symbols of their religion at school. There are other ways in which a dress code policy may be deemed discriminatory. In Suffolk County, Virginia, the ACLU challenged a proposed dress code policy that would have banned "any clothing worn by a student that is not in keeping with a student's gender and causes a disruption and/or distracts others from the educational process or poses a health or safety concern." The ACLU argued that this policy opened the door for discrimination based upon gender or sexual orientation and placed the blame for disruption on the victims rather than the students who chose to harass them for their clothing choices.

Title IX is a law that was passed in 1972 that prohibits gender discrimination in educational activities, including sports. Public schools are not allowed to segregate classes based upon gender. Sports teams may be gender specific as long as the opportunity to play a specific sport is offered to both boys and girls. For instance, it is legal for a school to operate separate boys' and girls' football or basketball teams. However, it is illegal for a school to prohibit a girl from joining a boys' team if a girls' team is not established. A school must also provide equal facilities, funding, transportation, coaching, practice time, and scheduling of games to boys teams and girls teams. If your school does not provide equal opportunities in sports to both genders, then it is in

Title IX guarantees that girls in high school will be given the same sports opportunities as their male schoolmates. This photo shows girls playing in a flag football championship in Boca Raton, Florida.

CONSTANCE MCMILLEN FOUGHT DISCRIMINATION AGAINST LGBT STUDENTS

During the 2009–2010 school year, a student named Constance McMillen made headlines when she fought against discrimination she experienced at Itawamba Agricultural High School in Fulton, Mississippi. Constance's desire was simple: she wanted to attend the prom with her significant other, a right that is exercised by countless high school students every year. However, because Constance is a lesbian and wanted to wear a tux to prom and attend with her girlfriend, the school prohibited her from doing so. Constance was told that if she and her girlfriend tried to attend the school-sponsored prom, they would be "ejected."

Constance did not take this news lightly. She enlisted the help of the American Civil Liberties Union, which sent a letter to the school threatening legal action if Constance and her girlfriend were not allowed to attend the prom. In response, the school canceled the official prom and encouraged students and parents to organize a prom independently. Constance and her ACLU lawyers went to court to challenge this decision, and the judge ruled that Constance must be allowed to attend the private prom that was being organized.

Although Constance was not explicitly prohibited from attending the private prom, she was not invited, and organizers made sure that she had trouble finding information about it. The private prom was canceled, but it was replaced by two different events: one at a country club, to which Constance was invited, and another several miles away, which the majority of the students attended.

The event to which Constance was invited was attended by only seven students. It seems that this was used as an opportunity to discriminate against several students who did not fit in with Itawamba High School's mainstream social scene. According to Constance, some of the few other attendees were students with learning difficulties. "They had the time of their lives," Constance told the *Advocate*. "That's the one good thing that came out of this, [these kids] didn't have to worry about people making fun of them [at their prom]."

Since the event itself, several other good things have come from Constance's courageous fight. She and the ACLU generated great publicity for her cause, including lots of media attention and a Facebook page called "Let Constance Take Her Girlfriend To Prom," which garnered hundreds of thousands of fans and continues to advocate for LGBT equality. Constance received a college scholarship from an anonymous donor. In 2010, she was awarded $35,000 in damages from the suit that she eventually filed against the school district.

High school senior Constance McMillen became a poster girl for LGBT student rights when she was denied the right to take her girlfriend to prom and fought back.

More importantly, the lawsuit resulted in the requirement that the district adopt a policy that prohibits discrimination

(continued on the next page)

(continued from the previous page)

against students based on sexual orientation. Because of Constance's courage and persistence and the legal support provided by the ACLU, future LGBT students in her district will be protected from the discrimination Constance experienced. Her story shows that students are not powerless when they are treated unfairly. Students can take action against discriminatory policies. There are organizations that will help, and there are judges who are moving the law forward with their decisions on LGBT issues.

violation of Title IX, and you can and should challenge its discriminatory policies.

LGBT STUDENTS AND DISCRIMINATION

Although discrimination on the basis of sexual orientation is not yet explicitly prohibited under federal law, hate crimes based on sexual orientation are punishable as a federal offense. In addition, a large number of states have laws explicitly prohibiting discrimination based on sexual orientation. LGBT students have many legal options for challenging discriminatory policies.

The ACLU has launched several campaigns to advocate for the rights of LGBT students. One of these campaigns, called Don't Filter Me, argues that LGBT students' First Amendment rights are violated when schools use website filtering software that blocks the websites of positive LGBT organizations while allowing access to anti-LGBT websites. While a school may block websites that contain sexually explicit material, it may not block non-sexual websites that provide support and positive information to LGBT students. To do so is a blatant act of discrimination.

LGBT students have the same right to free speech and expression as other students. If someone at school tries to silence you or prohibit you from speaking about your sexual orientation or your political views regarding LGBT issues, they are violating your right to free speech, and you have a right to challenge them. LGBT students and their allies also have the right to organize clubs, such as gay-straight alliances, to provide support and awareness in the school environment. In addition, if your school allows students to attend dances as couples, but it does not allow same-sex couples to attend, you may be able to challenge this policy as discriminatory, especially if sexual orientation is a protected category in your state.

When discriminatory actions by students toward other students are classified as bullying, they often carry more serious consequences. Several states include sexual orientation as a protected category under their anti-bullying laws. (Later, there will be a discussion of bullying and consequences in more detail.)

As with most aspects of students' rights, identifying and challenging discriminatory policies often requires research and interpretation of the existing laws. It also requires knowing the specific laws in your state, as many states provide additional legal protection to that which is included in the Constitution. The ACLU provides many resources for doing this research, as do some of the other organizations and publications mentioned at the end of this book.

CHAPTER 3

FAIR DISCIPLINE AND SECOND CHANCES: PRIVACY RIGHTS AND THE RIGHTS OF JUVENILE OFFENDERS

Another important area in which students need to be aware of their rights is that of school discipline. You need to know your legal rights regarding actions such as locker searches, the seizure of property, being questioned by the police, and drug and alcohol testing. You should also keep your right to freedom from discrimination in mind. While disciplinary policies are necessary, they cannot be used to target specific students. For instance, in many states, schools are allowed to install metal detectors. However, they are not allowed to require some students, but not others, to walk through those metal detectors. Unfortunately, in some cases, school discipline policies have been known to disproportionately target African-American and Latino youth, especially males. If you feel that you are being unfairly targeted due to your race, gender, or some other characteristic, you have every right to speak up and request the assistance of a parent, guidance counselor, or another adult that you trust. The rest of this chapter will provide an overview of your rights regarding common occurrences related to

Northwestern High School in Flint, Michigan, like many other urban high schools, requires its students to walk through metal detectors before entering. Pictured here is student Claressa Shields, Olympic gold medalist in women's middleweight boxing, who must pass through the metal detector as any other student would.

school discipline. Keep in mind that although school officials can and must do certain things to maintain order, they should do their best to do these things without violating students' constitutional rights.

SEARCH AND SEIZURE

Obviously, school officials have a responsibility to create and maintain a safe environment for all students. This means that they must sometimes conduct searches for things like drugs or weapons. However, students still have the right to a certain amount of privacy, and school officials have an obligation to follow the proper procedures when conducting searches. Although the Constitution does not explicitly mention privacy, the Supreme Court has confirmed that certain amendments imply this right. The Fourth Amendment states that government officials must have "probable cause" to search or seize a citizen's property. This means that they must have

A police officer and narcotics dog search student lockers. While the police must have a warrant to search your property, lockers are often considered school property and may be searched by school officials if they have evidence of a violation of the law or school rules.

some kind of reason to suspect that the person has committed a crime.

In school, although your constitutional rights generally still apply, the question of privacy is kind of tricky. As with many other issues, the specific laws that govern the procedures for search and seizure of property vary from state to state. While the police need a warrant to search your property, school officials do not. In a 1985 case called *New Jersey v. T.L.O.*, the Supreme Court ruled that school officials may search a student's property if they have "reasonable grounds for suspecting that the search will turn up evidence that the student has violated ... either the law or the rules of the school." However, as the ACLU website points out, this does not mean that the school can search your property simply because they believe that some student has committed an offense; they must have evidence that you personally committed the offense in question. While some states consider lockers to be school property and therefore open to searches, others consider them private because the items inside belong to the student. Your local ACLU can advise you regarding the specific policies about locker searches in your state.

Drug and alcohol tests are legally considered searches, so they are governed by the same rules as searches. However, the laws vary from state to state regarding how much reasonable evidence school officials must have before requiring you to take a test. If you feel you are being unfairly asked to undergo drug or alcohol testing, it is always an option to request the presence of your parents or a lawyer before the procedure continues.

NEW YORK CITY DEPARTMENT OF EDUCATION AND *J.G. v. MILLS*

The New York City Department of Education (DOE) has very specific guidelines about the ways the school system must help juvenile offenders transition back into school. However, this was not always the case. In 2004, because of complaints from many juvenile offenders and their families about the ways that the DOE handled this process, two organizations, The Legal Aid Society and Advocates for Children of New York, brought a class-action suit against the DOE. This case, called *J.G. v. Mills*, addressed a group of students, ages seven to twenty-one, who had been involved with the courts in one way or another and who were entitled to an education. The suit claimed that these students had been routinely denied the right to re-enroll in school or had been placed in disciplinary "alternative schools" that segregated them from the general student population and did not provide the same level of instruction. It also claimed that court-involved students who were entitled to special-education services often did not receive those services while detained or when they returned to school.

This case was not settled with the NYC Department of Education until April 2011, but when it was finally settled, the city agreed to a number of guidelines that specify how juvenile offenders returning to school should be treated. These guidelines state that students returning from any type of detention facility have the following rights:

> › The right to return to school in a timely manner following their return to the community. The guidelines specify that students must be placed in a school within five days of the date when they appear at a DOE enrollment office.

> › The right to any and all special-education services specified if the student has an IEP (Individualized Education Plan).

> › The right to help with transferring records and re-enrolling. This means that the DOE must help the student transfer records of the education he or she received while in the detention facility to the school where he or she is transferring. The DOE must assist with the re-enrollment process to make sure that the transition happens as quickly and smoothly as possible.

While these guidelines are specific to New York City schools, the general principle applies to juvenile offenders in any state. Just because you are in a detention facility, you do not lose your right to an education or to any special-education services to which you are entitled. Juvenile detention facilities are supposed to be focused on rehabilitating offenders, and education is a big part of that. In addition, when you leave the facility, you are entitled to return to school. If you encounter difficulties when trying to re-enroll, contact your local ACLU chapter to find out about the laws in your state and to seek assistance getting back into school. Being a juvenile offender does not mean that you lose your right to a free public education.

Police officers are often present in schools, especially in urban areas, so it is important to know that you have the right to remain silent if an officer questions you. This same right applies if a teacher or another school official questions you. If you think that you are being accused of a crime, you can and should choose to remain silent and request the presence of your parents *and* a lawyer before you speak. If you choose to speak without an adult present to represent you, the things you say can be used as evidence against you.

EDUCATIONAL RIGHTS OF JUVENILE OFFENDERS

When teens are convicted of crimes and placed in juvenile detention centers, they are entitled to an education while they are incarcerated. However, juvenile offenders placed in adult facilities sometimes receive no education whatsoever. The educational facilities in juvenile detention centers are often substandard and do not provide adequate instruction to keep students at grade level and allow them to keep up with their peers.

What happens when a juvenile offender is released from a detention center and returns to school? This varies from state to state and from school to school, but regardless of the specifics, it is never an easy transition. Youths returning to their communities after being incarcerated often have a difficult time readjusting. Different states have various programs that attempt to help juvenile offenders reenter their schools and communities and help them to avoid recidivism, which occurs when offenders return to the justice system for offenses similar to those for which they were originally convicted.

Virginia has an extensive set of guidelines to help juvenile offenders with reentry into the school system. These guidelines are drawn from research, experience, and advice of youth advocates, parents, detention centers, schools, and formerly incarcerated youths themselves. Virginia's guidelines describe in detail the roles of the agencies that are involved in guiding students through this transition. These guidelines mandate that released juvenile offenders must enroll in school immediately, and that they must be placed in classes that match their educational level. They also indicate that the families and the students themselves must be involved in the re-enrollment process. They recommend that individualized plans be developed for each reentering student.

Maine has put a law in place that requires the assembly of a "reintegration team" to help juvenile offenders with the transition back into the school environment. This team works to coordinate between the detention facility that the student is leaving, the administration at the school he or she is entering, and their family, teachers, and guidance counselor. This team is established as soon as the youth is given a release date to ensure that the transition is smooth and immediate.

CHAPTER 4

SEPARATE IS NOT EQUAL: THE RIGHT TO QUALITY EDUCATION FOR ALL STUDENTS

In the United States, all students are guaranteed the right to a free public education. Ideally, this should mean that all students in public schools receive the same quality of education, regardless of their race, thei socioeconomic status, or the location of their school. In 1954, the landmark Supreme Court case *Brown v. the Board of Education* ruled that segregation was unconstitutional. Prior to that ruling, black students and white students attended separate schools. After *Brown v. Board*, it became illegal for schools to be racially segregated. In legal terms, this means that de jure segregation (segregation mandated by law) was outlawed. However, the ruling in *Brown v. Board* could not comprehensively deal with de facto segregation.

De facto segregation occurs when a school or school district is not segregated by law, but remains segregated because the people who reside in the school's area belong primarily to one race. Often, schools in inner-city areas are primarily attended by black and/or Latino students, while schools in suburban areas are primarily attended by white students. Even though these schools are not legally segregated, following the *Brown v. Board* ruling, some school districts and schools were mandatorily integrated because their residential population results in de facto segregation. In the 1970s and 1980s, busing plans were put into place to counteract de facto segregation. Under these plans, students were transported by bus into school districts outside of their residential areas in an attempt to integrate the schools.

De facto segregation is still a problem in the United States today. In the book *Whistling Vivaldi and Other Clues To How Stereotypes Affect Us*, author Claude Steele discusses the

Pictured here are the plaintiffs in the landmark Supreme Court case Brown v. the Board of Education of Topeka, *which overturned the "separate but equal" doctrine, making racial segregation in schools illegal.*

33

fact that American public schools have actually been resegregating in recent years. He mentions how the populations of neighborhoods affect the populations of schools, saying "without desegregation plans, schools become as segregated as the neighborhoods that feed them. And those neighborhoods remain dramatically segregated, especially for whites." Steele also points out that in the 2000 census, neighborhoods were statistically shown to be highly segregated. Noteworthy figures were that "the average white American lives in a neighborhood that is 80 percent white and 7 percent black." Conversely, the average black American's neighborhood is "33 percent white and 51 percent black." Steele draws an outstanding conclusion from these figures, stating: "If you wanted to rearrange most U.S. cities so that race played no role in where people lived, you would have to move 85 percent of the black population.

The Supreme Court ruled long ago that "separate but equal" was a contradictory statement, and that a segregated school system was not an equitable one. This means that if our school system is still segregated, even if that segregation is no longer mandated by law, there is still a lot of work to be done toward achieving equality. Until that equality is achieved, many students will not receive the quality of education that is afforded to them by their constitutional rights.

SCHOOL CHOICE: VOUCHERS AND CHARTER SCHOOLS

There are many differing opinions about how to achieve true educational equity. The specific methods for creating an equitable school system are constantly debated. Among the most controversial issues are vouchers and charter schools.

Vouchers are certificates of funding given to parents by the government. Vouchers may be used toward a child's tuition in a private school if the parents opt not to send their child to the public school in his or her neighborhood. Supporters of vouchers argue that they provide low-income families with the resources to send their children to better schools. Critics argue that vouchers take funding away

There is debate across the country regarding the benefits and detriments of charter schools. Pictured here is New York governor Andrew Cuomo speaking at a rally in support of charter schools.

from public schools, diminishing the quality for those students whose parents do not or cannot take advantage of voucher programs.

Charter schools, or schools that receive public funding but are operated by independent entities other than the state, are another controversial issue in educational equity. Many charter schools set up shop in low-income neighborhoods, claiming to offer better opportunities to local children than those offered by the public schools in their district. The reality is that the quality of education, as well as the educational philosophies that guide charter schools, vary greatly. While some charter schools actually do provide better opportunities for their students, some are elitist, overly disciplinary, or otherwise flawed. Charter schools are not necessarily different from or better than public schools. The laws governing charter schools and their funding vary from state to state, so the effect they have on the public schools in each state varies as well.

Some people believe that vouchers and charter schools increase educational equity by offering parents and students more choices in the schools that students may attend. Other people, however, believe that this increased equity is an illusion, and that vouchers and charter schools harm public education by taking away funding and decreasing the quality of materials and instruction that public schools can provide. The debate regarding these issues is passionate on both sides.

STUDENTS WITH DISABILITIES

Another group of students who receive necessary protection under the law are students with disabilities. There are many students who fall into this category, with disabilities ranging from physical, such as using a wheelchair, to mental, such as language-processing disorders, to behavioral, such as conduct disorder or oppositional-defiant disorder.

There was a time when students with disabilities, especially those with physical or mental conditions that were perceived to severely limit their functioning, were often secreted away in special schools or institutions. Often, these facilities simply served as holding cells. There was no attempt made to educate the students, to

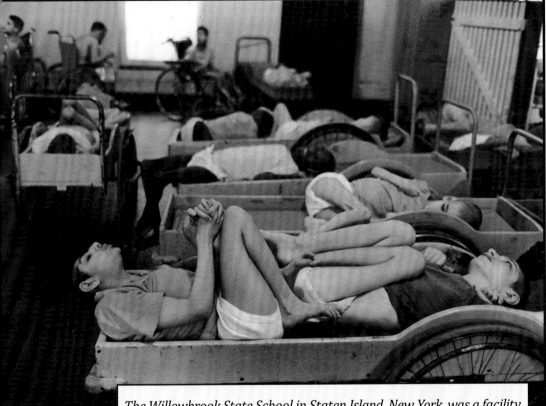

The Willowbrook State School in Staten Island, New York, was a facility for students with disabilities. It was shut down in the 1980s after being exposed for overcrowding, unsanitary conditions, and abuse.

emphasize their abilities, or to build upon those abilities to help them become more functional.

The most infamous of these schools was called Willowbrook State School, located on Staten Island, a borough of New York City. Not only was education at this "school" neglected, its students were subjected to terrible, overcrowded, unsanitary conditions, and to physical and sexual abuse. These conditions came to the public's attention in the mid-1970s, largely because of a televised exposé conducted by Geraldo Rivera, entitled

NICK JEWITT: AN INDIVIDUAL STORY

Nick Jewitt, a fifteen-year-old seventh grader in a suburban school district, is one of the students profiled in the book *Exceptional Lives: Special Education in Today's Schools*. Nick has several social and learning difficulties, including Asperger syndrome (an autism spectrum disorder), cerebral palsy, and obsessive-compulsive disorder. The one that causes him the most difficulty, however, is intermittent-explosive disorder, which causes him to burst into rages when he experiences frustration or when teachers and other school officials do not listen to his needs regarding what helps him to learn and what hinders him. Because of these rages, Nick has been removed from several schools, and some teachers have refused to teach him, or have tried to discipline him with yelling, threats, and physical restraint.

Although Nick's rages, and the rages of other students like him, can be distracting and frightening to teachers, administrators, and other students, Nick has the right to receive an education. He also has the right to be taught in the least restrictive environment possible, and because he has an IEP (individualized education plan), he has the right to certain accommodations to help him learn and succeed.

The administrators and teachers who have helped Nick to succeed are the ones who have recognized his rights under IDEA (Individuals with Disabilities Education Act). Rather than dealing with him in a strictly disciplinary manner or relegating him to a "special school," they have worked with him and his mother to figure out ways to help him. Some of the things that have helped include letting him store his books in the classroom rather than his locker (because his cerebral palsy makes walking more difficult and slows him down), letting him use the faculty elevator, and letting him use a calculator in math class (though he cannot use it on state examinations). Nick often has to miss class to attend appointments with various professionals such as speech therapists, psychologists, psychiatrists, and cerebral palsy specialists, and his teachers allow him to make up the work he misses on those days.

Because of the assistance and understanding he receives at his current school, Nick has made significant progress. He is enrolled in three honors classes, and his explosive episodes occur much less frequently. He has a career goal: after high school, he wants to attend college and enter the information-technology profession.

Nick's story shows how important it is for the rights of students with disabilities to be respected. When Nick was treated strictly as a disciplinary case, his explosions became worse rather than better. However, when his rights under IDEA were respected, and he was given the accommodations he needed, they became less frequent and he became more successful. This shows that IDEA's requirements can make things much better for students with disabilities.

Willowbrook: The Last Great Disgrace. The school was finally closed for good in 1987.

INDIVIDUALS WITH DISABILITIES EDUCATION ACT

The law that governs the rights of students with disabilities is called the Individuals with Disabilities Education Act, or IDEA. It was originally put into effect by Congress in 1965 to ensure that students with disabilities were entitled to a free public education, like all other students. Over the years, it has been amended to include other provisions, including the requirement that students with disabilities be placed in the "least restrictive environment" possible. It also specifies that any student who is diagnosed with special needs must have an IEP, or Individualized Education Plan. This plan is different for every student and specifies the services to which he or she is entitled, such as receiving one-on-one instruction, having extra time to complete tests, or sitting in a specific area of the room. The IEP also includes goals for the student's progress, which are changed and updated periodically. IEPs are developed by a team that includes the student's parents, a general-education teacher, a special-education teacher, a school official who supervises the special-education program, an interpreter (if needed), and, when appropriate, the student him- or herself.

CHAPTER 5

FREEDOM FROM BULLYING AND HARASSMENT: THE RIGHT TO FEEL SAFE AND COMFORTABLE AT SCHOOL

In recent years, more and more people have spoken up about the fact that students have the right to attend school without being harassed, for any reason, by teachers, staff, or other students. Harassment by other students often occurs in the form of bullying. The Stop Bullying website defines bullying as "unwanted, aggressive behavior among school-aged children that involves a real or perceived power imbalance. The behavior is repeated, or has potential to be repeated, over time." The website goes on to specify that a power imbalance can appear in many different forms, "such as physical strength, access to embarrassing information, or popularity." When any of these factors is used to intimidate or harass someone, it qualifies as bullying.

Three different types of bullying have been identified: verbal bullying, social/relational bullying, and physical bullying. Examples of verbal bullying include writing mean or manipulative notes, making threats, taunting, and directing sexual innuendoes at someone. Examples of social/relational bullying include purposely ostracizing someone, telling others to leave someone out, spreading rumors, and deliberately

Bullying is not limited to physical violence. Antibullying policies also cover verbal bullying and social or relational bullying, such as the type of exclusion and harassment being directed at the boy in this picture.

embarrassing someone. Examples of physical bullying include hitting or kicking someone, taking or breaking someone's things, spitting, and making rude gestures.

Cyberbullying is a type of verbal social bullying that takes place through electronic means, such as text messages, instant messages, and social media. It can include spreading damaging rumors via the Internet, posting embarrassing pictures, and sending threatening or harassing messages. A student who is bullied at school often has a break from his or her tormenters when school is over, but cyberbullying follows its targets home, sometimes even into their bedrooms, via cell

DATING AND LEGAL ISSUES

Bullying isn't the only interaction between students at schools where legal consequences might arise. Dating, flirting, sexual activity between students is another area where the law comes into play. Legal issues might not be the first thing you think about in relation to dating. However, it is important to note the potential legal consequences of certain dating situations you might encounter, especially in school. To protect both yourself and the people you date, you should be informed about what is and isn't legal.

A major legal issue related to high school dating is statutory rape, which is a general term used to refer to sexual intercourse in which one of the partners is below the legal age of consent required to engage in sexual activity. You probably already know that it is illegal for a teacher, coach, or other adult to engage in a sexual relationship with a student. However, there are certain situations in which sex could be a legal violation even if it occurs between two students. In this situation, rape does not require any kind of force. Because the person under the age of consent is considered too young to make the decision for him- or herself, it is considered rape even if both partners consented. This is true even if the younger partner initiated the encounter.

For instance, if a freshman and an eighteen-year-old senior have sex, and the freshman is below the age of consent, the senior could be legally prosecuted in many states. In thirty-four of the fifty states, the legal age of consent is sixteen, an age that many students don't reach until their junior year. The details of the laws governing statutory rape vary from state to state. If you are considering having sex and there is an age difference between you and your partner, you should research the applicable laws for your state. Oftentimes, statutory rape is determined not just by the age of the younger party, but the age of the younger party in relation to the age of the older party. Sometimes if the age difference between the two parties is minimal (for

(continued on the next page)

(continued from the previous page)

example, an eighteen-year-old and a fifteen-year-old that are only three years apart), this closeness in age can be used as a valid legal defense, even though one party is over eighteen and the other is a minor.

Another legal issue related to dating is that of sexting or sending explicit pictures online or over the phone. When you are dating someone, you might be tempted to send explicit photos of yourself, or to ask your significant other to send explicit pictures to you. Although you might already know that it is illegal for adults to receive or distribute explicit photos of children, you might be unaware that it is also illegal for minors to receive or distribute explicit photos of themselves or other minors. This means that if you exchange a nude photo with your significant other, even if it is only meant to be shared between the two of you, you could be putting yourselves at risk for legal consequences.

Finally, a major issue with sexting or sending and receiving explicit photos of other students is the possibility that these explicit messages or photos could lead to bullying. Oftentimes, partners will redistribute explicit photos without permission, especially after the couple breaks up. Although this redistribution would be considered criminal and the culprit would likely face legal consequences, this situation can best be avoided by not sending or redistributing explicit photos, even with a trusted partner.

phones and computers. This is one reason why cyberbullying can be particularly damaging.

Because of a rash of suicides due to bullying that have appeared in the news over the past decade, this topic has received a lot of attention in recent years. Although there is no federal law that applies specifically to bullying, many states have developed laws to regulate this type of behavior. Every state except Montana has passed some kind of anti-bullying legislation. In addition, if bullying is based on race, religion,

You do not have to tolerate bullying or harassment. If you are being bullied, reach out to a teacher, a counselor, or another trusted adult. It is the school's legal responsibility to take action.

national origin, color, disability, or gender, it is covered under the categories that are protected from harassment by the Constitution.

There are many reasons a student might be at risk for being bullied. Anyone who is different can become a target. Some of these reasons include appearance, weight, socioeconomic status, being new at school, or being considered annoying. One group that is particularly targeted for bullying is students who identify (or are perceived to identify) as lesbian, gay, bisexual, or transgender. Many of the young

NEW JERSEY ANTI-BULLYING BILL OF RIGHTS ACT

New Jersey is one of the states that has taken bullying the most seriously and developed some of the most comprehensive anti-bullying legislation. During the 2011–2012 school year, the Anti-Bullying Bill of Rights Act went into effect in New Jersey schools. This law defines bullying as "any gesture, any written, verbal or physical act, or any electronic communication, whether it be a single incident or series of incidents, that is reasonably perceived as being motivated either by any actual or perceived characteristic ... that takes place on school property, at any school-sponsored function, on a school bus, or off school grounds ... that substantially disrupts or interferes with the orderly operation of the school or the rights of other students, and that a reasonable person should know, under the circumstances, will have the effect of physically or emotionally harming a student or damaging a student's property, or placing a student in reasonable fear of physical or emotional harm to his person or damage his property."

The law includes detailed requirements for reporting and addressing bullying behavior:

› School employees and contracted service providers are required to report to the principal any acts of bullying that they witness or about which they receive reliable information. They must also file a written report within two days.

› The principal must inform the parents or guardians of the student who is bullied and must inform them of available counseling and other interventions.

› The principal must initiate or designate someone to initiate an investigation into the incident, to be handled by the school's anti-bullying specialist, which each school must have.

› This investigation must be completed as soon as possible and no more than ten days after the principal was initially informed of the incident. The anti-bullying specialist may make changes to the original written report.

› Within two days after the investigation is completed, the superintendent must receive the written report. The superintendent may take appropriate actions including ordering counseling, establishing training programs, or imposing discipline.

› At the first school board meeting after the investigation, the board must receive the report along with details about the actions taken to address the incident.

› The parents of the students involved (both the bully(s) and the student(s) being bullied, are entitled to information regarding the investigation, and they may also request a hearing with the school board in which the anti-bullying specialist can participate. At the next board meeting, the school board must issue a written decision that either accepts, rejects, or modifies the superintendent's original decision. If the involved parties are unhappy with the board's decision, they may appeal to the commissioner of education.

› Twice a year, New Jersey school districts must submit their reports on bullying to both the public and the Department of Education. The department will assign a grade to each district based on these reports, which must be posted on the district website.

Although not all states have such extensive and specific laws in place regarding bullying, more and more states are adopting comprehensive laws and policies. New Jersey's example may provide a framework for other states as they develop their own ways of handling this serious issue.

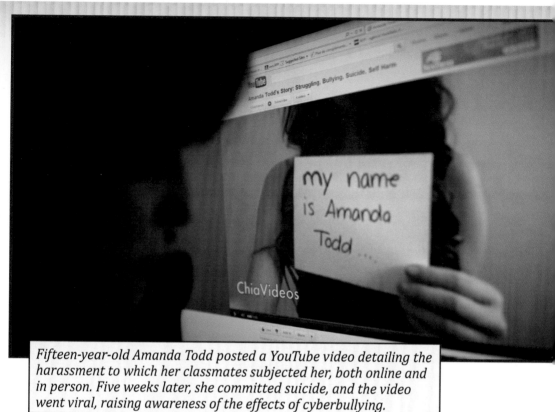

Fifteen-year-old Amanda Todd posted a YouTube video detailing the harassment to which her classmates subjected her, both online and in person. Five weeks later, she committed suicide, and the video went viral, raising awareness of the effects of cyberbullying.

people whose suicides have made the news recently have been members of this group, such as Tyler Clementi, a freshman at Rutgers University, who committed suicide in 2010 after his roommate posted about Clementi's homosexual encounter on Twitter, and Jadin Bell, a gay thirteen-year-old boy who had been bullied extensively both at school and online. Although sexual orientation is not included in the categories protected from harassment under the Constitution, many states, including New York, New Jersey, Oregon, and Washington, have specifically included sexual orientation in their anti-bullying laws.

Students with special needs—such as physical disabilities, epilepsy, speech impediments, or ADHD—are also often targeted for bullying. If bullying is specifically related to a student's disability, it is a violation of federal law. If the school is aware of the harassment and neglects to address it, then the school is also in violation of the law.

EFFECTS AND CONSEQUENCES OF BULLYING

If you are being bullied, you should report it to someone immediately. The effects of bullying can be serious and long-lasting. Students who are continuously bullied are more likely to suffer from depression, anxiety, and other mental health problems. Bullying can also contribute to substance abuse and decreased academic achievement. You have the right to protect yourself from these things, whether or not the law explicitly covers the type of bullying you are experiencing. Speak to your teacher, guidance counselor, or another adult at school whom you trust. If you do not feel comfortable speaking to school staff yourself, then confide in your parents, and ask them to intervene. You should not have to suffer, and your bully or bullies should not get away with these violations.

What happens when bullying is reported varies based upon the school and the specific situation. Many forms of bullying are handled within the school itself. School officials may interview both the victim and the bully to gather as much information about the incident as they can and document it through an incident report. This might result in anything from a verbal warning to a suspension, or possibly even expulsion, for the bully. Generally, the consequences increase the more a behavior is repeated. If you are caught bullying once or twice and change your behavior, you might be able to avoid consequences that will affect your life in the long run. However, the longer you continue the behavior, the more you run the risk of damaging your own future.

Because cyberbullying is considered a special category in many states, the consequences of this type of bullying are often more severe and may include intervention by police. Stopbullying.gov specifies that cyberbullying, which includes threats of violence, sexually explicit photos or messages, photos or videos filmed in private places such as bathrooms or locker rooms, stalking, or hate crimes, should be reported to law enforcement in addition to being reported to the school. If you are a student who engages in any of these behaviors, you should be aware that your choices could have serious legal consequences. In some states, cyberbullying that is classified as harassment can result in criminal charges and even jail time.

Crimes that occur over the Internet can carry harsh penalties, and they often result in the participants being charged with a felony and tried as adults. Lawyers have a particularly difficult time defending against these charges, because when something is done online, it leaves a virtual "paper trail," a record of the crime that can be accessed again and again. This is similar to cases for crimes involving texting or other phone records. Think twice before doing or saying anything online or on social media platforms that could possibly be construed as harassment. The consequences could be severe, no matter how frivolous your intentions.

GLOSSARY

advocate To speak or write in favor of a cause.

busing The practice of sending students by bus into a school that is outside their district in order to integrate the school.

class-action suit A suit in which either the plaintiff or the defendant is a group instead of an individual.

de jure segregation Segregation that is mandated by law.

de facto segregation Segregation that is not mandated by law, but occurs as a result of circumstances, such as residential patterns.

dissent To express as opinion or position that is different from the official, common, or popular one.

educational equity The measure of achievement, opportunity, and fairness in education.

IEP (individualized education plan) A customized plan developed for special-education students that specifies the services they are entitled to receive.

incarcerated Imprisoned or confined.

incite To stir up or encourage unlawful or violent behavior.

least restrictive environment The provision of IDEA (the Individuals with Disabilities Education

Act) that states that students with disabilities must be educated alongside their mainstream peers to the greatest extent possible.

ostracize To exclude someone from a group or society.

peaceable assembly The right to gather peacefully, as guaranteed by the First Amendment to the United States Constitution.

recidivism The tendency to relapse into criminal behavior and repeat previous, or similar, offenses.

recourse Help in a difficult situation.

rehabilitate To bring someone back to normal life after illness, prison, etc.

seize To take something by force.

socioeconomic Involving a combination of social and economic factors.

Title IX Part of the Education Amendments of 1972, which prohibits discrimination based upon gender in educational programs and activities.

FOR MORE INFORMATION

American Civil Liberties Union
125 Broad Street, 18th Floor
New York, NY 10004
(212) 549-2500
Website: http://www.aclu.org
Founded in 1920, the ACLU has worked for decades to gain, preserve, and protect the rights of groups that have been discriminated against. They fight for many different groups, including minorities, women, LGBTQ people, and students. They have branches in various states.

Canadian Multicultural Education Foundation
Unit #8, 2nd Floor
10575 114 Street
Edmonton, AB T5H 3J6
Canada
(780) 434-5568
Website: http://www.cmef.ca
Founded in 1990, CMEF works to educate the public and build awareness about the benefits of a multicultural society and to advocate for the human rights of all Canadians.

CASES
346 Broadway, 3rd Floor
New York, NY 10013
(212) 732-0076
Website: http://www.cases.org
CASES is a New York City organization that helps court-involved juvenile and adult offenders reenter society

after being incarcerated. The organization has many programs to help with reentry and also has programs that provide alternative forms of sentencing to help eligible offenders avoid incarceration.

Institute for Democratic Education in America
620 SW 5th Avenue, Suite 910
Portland, OR 97205
(800) 878-5740
Website: http://www.democraticeducation.org
IDEA is a nationwide organization that works to connect education with democratic values by developing alliances and sharing resources among innovative educators and organizations.

Ontario Coalition For Social Justice
15 Gervais Drive, Suite 305
Toronto, ON M3C 1Y8
Canada
(416) 441-3714
Website: http://www.ocsj.ca
Founded in 1985, OCSJ is dedicated to achieving equity in health care, education, and social services, and to human rights, including the rights of immigrants, undocumented workers, and refugees.

Rethinking Schools
1001 East Keefe Avenue
Milwaukee, WI 53212
(414) 964-9646

Website: http://www.rethinkingschools.org
Founded in 1986 in Milwaukee, Rethinking Schools is a nonprofit organization dedicated to fostering racial and class equity through school reform.

Southern Poverty Law Center
400 Washington Avenue
Montgomery, AL 36104
(334) 956-8200
Website: http://www.splcenter.org
Since 1971, the SPLC has worked and advocated for justice against hatred and bigotry. Founded by two civil rights lawyers, the organization tracks hate groups and provides educational materials and resources to aid the struggle for justice and equity in education, legal matters, and many other aspects of society.

WEBSITES

Because of the changing nature of Internet links, Rosen Publishing has developed an online list of websites related to the subject of this book. This site is updated regularly. Please use this link to access the list:

http://www.rosenlinks.com/KYR/Scho

FOR FURTHER READING

Cambron-McCabe, Nelda H. *Legal Rights of Teachers and Students* (3rd Edition). New York, NY: Pearson, 2013.

Chaltain, Sam. *Our School: Searching For Community in the Era of Choice.* New York, NY: Teachers College Press, 2014.

Cox, Steven M. *Juvenile Justice: A Guide to Theory, Policy and Practice.* Washington, DC: Sage Publications, 2010.

Cushman, Clare, and Melvin Urofsky. *Black, White and Brown: The Landmark School Desegregation Case.* Thousand Oaks, CA: CQ Press, 2004.

Hicks, Aubrey. *Students' Rights* (Debating the Issues). Pelham, NY: Benchmark, 2011.

Humes, Edward. *No Matter How Loud I Shout: A Year In the Life of Juvenile Court.* New York, NY: Simon and Schuster, 1997.

Jacobs, Thomas A. *Teen Cyberbullying Investigated: Where Do Your Rights End and Consequences Begin?* Minneapolis, MN: Free Spirit, 2010.

Jacobs, Thomas A. *What Are My Rights? Q&A About Teens and the Law.* Minneapolis, MN: Free Spirit, 2011.

Johnson, John W. *The Struggle for Student Rights: Tinker v. Des Moines and the 1960s.* Lawrence, KS: University Press of Kansas, 1997.

McCarthy, Martha M., Nelda H. Cambron-McCabe, and Suzanne E. Eckes. *Public School Law: Teachers' and Students' Rights* (7th Edition). New York, NY: Pearson, 2013.

Morgan, Iwan and Phillip Davies. *From Sit-Ins to SNCC: The Student Civil Rights Movement in the 1960s.* Gainesville, FL: University Press of Florida, 2013.

Perryman-Clark, Stacy, David E. Kirkland, and Austin Jackson. *Students' Right to Their Own Language.* Boston, MA: Bedford/St. Martin's, 2014.

Ramey, R. Chace. *Student First Amendment Speech and Expression Rights: From Armbands to Bong HiTS.* El Paso, TX: LFB Scholarly Publishing, 2011.

Rios, Victor. *Punished: Policing the Lives of Black and Latino Boys.* New York, NY: NYU Press, 2011.

Rothstein, Laura. *Special Education Law* (Fifth Edition). Washington, DC: Sage Publications, 2013.

Russo, Charles J. *The Legal Rights of Students with Disabilities.* Lanham, MD: Rowman and Littlefield, 2011.

Stokes, John A. *Students On Strike: Jim Crow, Civil Rights, Brown, and Me.* Washington, DC: National Geographic, 2008.

Warnick, Bryan R. *Understanding Student Rights in Schools: Speech, Religion, and Privacy in Educational Settings.* New York, NY: Teachers College Press, 2012.

Yim, Catherine Y. *The School-to-Prison Pipeline: Structuring Legal Reform.* New York, NY: NYU Press, 2012.

BIBLIOGRAPHY

ACLU. "Search and Seizure." Retrieved April 7, 2014 (https://www.aclu.org/criminal-law-reform/ search-and-seizure).

ACLU. "Your Right to Privacy." Retrieved April 7, 2014 (https://www.aclu.org/technology-and-liberty /your-right-privacy).

ACLU of Vermont. "Students Rights—Equal Protection and Discrimination." Retrieved April 5, 2014 (http:// www.acluvt.org/pubs/students_rights/equal _protection.php).

Advocates for Children of New York. "J.G. v. Mills." Retrieved April 6, 2014 (https://www.advocatesforchildren.org/ litigation/class_actions/jg_vs_mills).

Bill of Rights Institute. "First Amendment: Freedom of Assembly (1791)." Retrieved April 3, 2014 (http:// billofrightsinstitute.org/resources/educator -resources/americapedia/americapedia-bill-of -rights/first-amendment/freedom-of-assembly).

Broverman, Neal. "ACLU Investigates Fake Prom." *Advocate*, April 5, 2010. Retrieved April 2, 2014 (http://www. advocate.com/news/daily-news/2010 /04/05/aclu-investigating-fake-prom).

CNN Justice. "Mississippi School Pays Damages to Lesbian Teen Over Prom Dispute." July 20, 2010. Retrieved April 2, 2014 (http://www.cnn.com/2010/CRIME /07/20/mississippi.lesbian.settlement).

Cornell University Law School Legal Information Institute. "Brandenburg v. Ohio." Retrieved April 4, 2014 (http://www.law.cornell.edu/supremecourt/text /395/444).

Cornell University Law School Legal Information Institute. "14th Amendment." Retrieved April 3, 2014 (http://www.law.cornell.edu/constitution/amendmentxiv).

Cornell University Law School Legal Information Institute. "Tinker v. Des Moines Independent Community School Dist." Retrieved April 4, 2014 (http://www.law.cornell.edu/supremecourt/text/393/503).

FindLaw. "Cyberbullying." Retrieved April 5, 2014 (http://criminal.findlaw.com/criminal-charges/cyber-bullying.html).

HuffPost Gay Voices. "Jadin Bell Dead." *Huffington Post*, February 4, 2013. Retrieved April 2014 (http://www.huffingtonpost.com/2013/02/04/jadin-bell-dead-gay-oregon-teen-hanging_n_2617909.html).

National Archives. "Teaching With Documents: The Civil Rights Act of 1964 and the Equal Employment Opportunity Commission." Retrieved April 5, 2014 (http://www.archives.gov/education/lessons/civil-rights-act).

Rivera, Geraldo. *Willowbrook: The Last Great Disgrace.* WABC-TV, 1972.

See You at the Pole. "See You at the Pole FAQ." Retrieved April 2, 2014 (http://syatp.com/syatpstore/index.php?option=com_content&view=article&id=28&Itemid=37#4).

The Sentencing Project. "Youth Reentry Fact Sheet." Retrieved April 6, 2014 (http://www.sentencingproject.org/doc/publications/jj_youthreentryfactsheet.pdf).

Steele, Claude. *Whistling Vivaldi and Other Clues to How Stereotypes Affect Us*. New York: W.W. Norton & Co., 2010.

StopBullying.gov. "Bullying Definition." Retrieved April 6, 2014 (http://www.stopbullying.gov/what-is-bullying/definition/index.html).

Turnbull, Ann. *Exceptional Lives: Special Education in Today's Schools* (7th Edition). New York, NY: Pearson, 2012.

Women's Sports Foundation. "Myth Busting: What Every Female Athlete Should Know. " Retrieved April 6, 2014 (https://www.womenssportsfoundation.org/en/home/athletes/for-athletes/know-your-rights/athlete-resources/mythbusting-what-every-female-athlete-should-know).

INDEX

ABOUT THE AUTHOR

Rebecca T. Klein was born in Detroit, Michigan. She writes books for young adults and has a master's degree in English education from Brooklyn College. She has worked as a counselor and director in various youth programs, taught English as a Second Language in South Korea, and worked as a substitute teacher in NYC schools. All of her work is driven by her lifelong commitment to anti-racism and social justice.

ABOUT THE EXPERT REVIEWER

Lindsay A. Lewis, Esq., is a practicing criminal defense attorney in New York City, where she handles a wide range of matters, from those discussed in this series to high-profile federal criminal cases. She believes that each and every defendant deserves a vigorous and informed defense. Ms. Lewis is a graduate of the Benjamin N. Cardozo School of Law and Vassar College.

PHOTO CREDITS